Parched
Soul
of
America

Leslie Kay Hedger
with Dr. David R. Reagan

Huntington House Publishers

Huntington House Publishers
P.O. Box 53788
Lafayette, Louisiana 70505

Library of Congress Card Catalog Number 94-079094
ISBN 1-56384-078-2

Dedication

Dedicated to
Jesus of Nazareth
the master assembler of words
and our Emancipator

Contents

Foreword

Dr. David R. Reagan

In 1980, the ministry I represent, Lamb & Lion, began broadcasting a radio program called "Christ in Prophecy." It soon became nationwide in scope. Over the years, the listeners have sent me many of their original poems. Although all of them were written in great sincerity and many contained very profound thoughts, very few exhibited any artistic merit. Good poetry is difficult to find, whether it be secular or spiritual in nature.

In the mid-80s, I received a sheaf of poems from the author of this book, Kay Hedger. I found out later that she had been listening to the ministry's radio program and felt that her poems were in agreement with our end-time emphasis on the soon return of Jesus.

A Wonderful Surprise

When I first received the poems, I put them aside without reading them, not suspecting what a gold mine of spiritual gems the Lord had placed in my hands. Several weeks later, when I picked them up again and started reading, I found that I could not put them down.

They were profoundly convicting, written with a true prophetic spirit. And, they were outstanding poetically. I recognized immediately that I held in my hands the product of a greatly gifted poet who was writing from a prophetic heart.

Over the years that followed, I read many of Kay's poems over the radio and used a number of them in our monthly prophetic newsletter. I tried repeatedly to urge her to put together a book of her poems, but I found her very reticent.

As I got to know her better, I came to realize that her reticence was an expression of humility. Although she roared like a lion in her poems, she was meek as a lamb when it came to any public recognition, always fearing that she might attract some attention that should go to the Lord. For example, she would have been perfectly happy with me using the poems and never even identifying her as their author!

The Origin of This Book

About a year ago, I began pressing Kay once again to express what the Lord was showing her about America. I felt a real urgency to get the burden of her heart into print. I prayed that the Lord would convict her that the time had come for her to take this important step. My prayers prevailed, and Kay overwhelmed me by submitting almost two hundred new poems that she had written in a burst of inspiration over a period of only three months! (Kay denies that she writes from "inspiration." As she puts it, "Most everything I write comes from God-ordained experience.")

What an incredible blessing it has been to read these poems, pray about them, meditate upon them, and seek the Lord for a way to present them to the public.

As I was working on the poems one evening, the Lord began to impress upon my heart a way in which to organize them. I thought of the apostle Paul's end-time prophecy in 2 Timothy 3:1-5 where he describes what society will be like in the end times. He says that the religion will be centered on man (humanism), the god will be money (materialism), the lifestyle will be the pursuit of pleasure (hedonism), and the result will be a society wallowing in despair (nihilism). The poems seemed to naturally fall into these categories.

Kay quickly agreed with this organizational concept, and we went to work trying to make the difficult, even agonizing, decisions as to which poems to include and which to lay aside. As we worked together, everything fell into place so neatly and smoothly that I came to realize that we were definitely working under a special anointing of the Spirit.

The Nature of the Poems

As you read these poems, you will find them easy to understand but difficult to swallow. They have a cutting edge that goes straight to the heart. They are convicting, and you may find yourself on your knees repenting and praying for yourself, your family, your church, and your country before you get finished with the book.

Keep in mind that God never pours out His wrath on any society without first providing warning through prophetic voices. He warned the world through Noah's preaching for 120 years. He warned Sodom and Gomorrah through Abraham. He called Ninevah to repentance, first through Jonah, and then again later through Nahum.

God is raising up prophetic voices all over America today to call this nation to repentance and to warn of destruction if we refuse to repent. Kay Hedger is one of those prophetic voices, speaking in poetry like the Old Testament prophets Isaiah and Hosea. Also, like those two prophets, she presents her thoughts in the form of a judicial indictment. You will find this same approach in Isaiah 5 and Hosea 4.

The Nature of God's Judgments

America is under judgment. Kay describes many of

those judgments in her poems. God uses judgments, together with prophetic voices, to call a nation to repentance. When the people steadfastly refuse to repent, the nation finally reaches a point where its "wound is incurable" (Nahum 3:19 and Jeremiah 30:12), and the Lord moves it from judgment to destruction.

If America continues to refuse to repent, its ultimate destruction will be beyond anything we can possibly imagine, for those to whom much is given, much is expected (Luke 12:48). We have been blessed as no other nation in history since the time of Judah. In our unparalleled freedom, we have been saturated with God's Word and the gospel. Unlike the Russian people, we have no excuse before God. Yet, consider what the Lord did to the Soviet Empire, reducing it overnight from superpower status to the level of a Third World poverty stricken country. Do we have reason to expect gentler treatment? I think not.

The Nature of God's Prophetic Voices

I never cease to be amazed at the people God calls to speak His prophetic warnings. In Old Testament times, He used an incredible variety of people, from the erudite Isaiah to the uneducated Amos, from the unknown Joel to the famous King David, from the courageous Daniel to the cowardly Jonah. The only thing they all seem to have had in common is a heart for God.

God continues to work in those same mysterious ways today because He "has chosen the foolish things of the world to shame the wise, and God has chosen the weak things of the world to shame the things which are strong" (1 Corinthians 1:27).

A Contemporary Prophetic Voice

Kay Hedger grew up on a small southern Illinois

farm. After marrying her high school sweetheart, she worked for the government in civil service positions while her husband, Richard, served in the military. Moving to Texas in the early '70s, they started their family, and Kay made the commitment to stay home with her children.

In 1980, she became aware of the moral decline of American society and began writing "letters of frustration" to God. This writing unexpectedly took the form of poetry and a calling to stand in the gap for her nation. Never having studied poetry, Kay does not consider herself to be a poet, but rather a seeker of truth.

She is the mother of two adult daughters. She and her husband reside in the "piney woods" of East Texas.

Prepare yourself now for a difficult spiritual feast. When you finish reading this book, you will understand fully the meaning of the following words which the Lord spoke to the prophet Ezekiel:

> I am sending you to them who are stubborn and obstinate children; and you shall say to them, "Thus says the Lord God." As for them, whether they listen or not—for they are a rebellious house—*they will know that a prophet has been among them.*
>
> —Ezekiel 2:4-5 (emphasis added)

Preface

Out of three months of intercession, come these poems—each written as if the blood of the nation were on my hands—each a prayer to loosen a stronghold of evil—each a fire burning in my spirit that would not be quenched until penned in ink.

May their mere existence be a deathblow to the forces of lucre, lust, and lethargy that threaten to destroy this, God's nation of ambassadors for righteousness. And, may The People, through the humiliation of repentance, see the resurrection of the TRUTH that sets men free.

Leslie Kay Hedger
May 1994

Christ
The Center of History

We pick and choose
heroes of time
and rewrite history
to fit political movements
and remove from memory
the Great Emancipator
whose life put man
into eternity

Introduction

England's reaction to the Boston Tea Party of 1773 was the imposition of what the colonists labeled "The Intolerable Acts." These acts were intended to punish America for resisting British control over her economic affairs. They were also designed to force America into submission to British rulership. This was the impetus that led to the war for America's independence. The colonists found themselves fighting on their own soil for the right to govern themselves.

The People of Freedom once again find themselves subject to an aristocracy—a leadership that operates independently of the will of The People. Fear of retribution by governing authorities prevents any effort to reclaim lost liberties. As a result, shameless liars, sent to lead, daily perform "intolerable acts" against the sovereign states, and The People lose confidence in the power of their vote.

The colonists left England in search of a place where they could live and worship free of government interference. That freedom, which was purchased with the blood of our ancestors, is now being jeopardized by a leadership that refuses to acknowledge the authority of God over the affairs of men. Americans must now call their leaders to accountability before God or surrender their sovereignty to the impersonal dictatorship of a political machine.

However, a nation in love with itself cannot entreat the mercy of a just God. A people who have forsaken purity of conscience dare not attempt to clean up city hall, lest they call down divine judgment upon an entire country in mutiny against its Creator. A nation is only as strong as the character of its people. May the cry of America, threatened by self-inflicted extinction, be:

> I lift up my soul to You
> I lay my sins at Your feet
> I cry aloud with my voice
> Deliver me—rescue me
> Save me from myself

ONE

Political Decadence

In the last days difficult times will come.
                                    —2 Timothy 3:1

Statism

The Great Sovereign Source

Our Father
which art the State
Blessed be Thy provision

Thy will be imposed
upon the will of The People
in each State
as it is in Washington

Give us each day
permission to exist
and forgive us our longings
for freedoms lost
and our reluctance to relinquish
our children to Socialism

Lead us not into poverty
but deliver us from capitalism
for By the State we are begotten
   For the State we are preserved
   Through the State we are made
     complete

Reinvented Government

Refusing to bow to a monarchy
America fought for the right
to govern herself
and won a government
that refuses to control itself

Snubbing its nose at the division of powers
meant to bridle evil intent
Congress "reinvents" government
making it partial
to a powerful elite

Moral Relativity

State of the Heart

A draft-dodging, drug "exhaling,"
sodomy protecting, shady dealing,
tax raising, child exploiting,
baby killing, feminist pandering,
religion robbing, border betraying,
gun confiscating, military reducing,
womanizer
becomes Commander-in-Chief
and the Nation gets a leader
who reflects the true condition
of its heart

Condemned From Within

Fools who say "there is no God"
weaken the foundation of the nation
by relinquishing our rights
to constitutional revisionists
who remove the "checks" upon will and appetite
and bow to a "dictator" religion
　　—the deity of man—

Using the Law to guarantee Libertarianism,
　　Promiscuity is promoted in schools
　　Sodomy is politically protected
　　Pornography is distributed to criminals
　　"Economic reforms" attack the family
　　Baby killing is made a privacy issue
　　The United Nations becomes our military
　　　　commander

Representatives labor in vain
to repair a house
"condemned for structural damage"
brought about by the denial
　　—of the sinful nature of man—

Abuse of Power

Identity Crisis
(Isaiah 3:12)

Coasting along
on a godly heritage
misleaders govern
as if there is no God
and defraud the people
with schemes of power

Liberated women
rule child-minded men
and mentor a generation
of cross-dressed, unisex,
tattooed, skinheaded,
Neo-Femi-Nazi delinquents

Who secretly long
to be shifted into gear
and given a divine
destiny

No Moral Consensus

By catering to civil libertarians
who sue the Church
for a godless government,
Congress legislates immorality
and creates a permissive society
with no roots

Power Failure

Authority structures
neglect
to hold back evil
and release oppression
upon The People
giving Satan full reign
in the land
and creating a climate
of mayhem

Political Hurdy-Gurdy

Men and women
with personal agendas
manipulate people
            programs
        and providence
using the public
as a crank
for their political machine

Stolen Virtue

A pack rat enters
the house by night
to steal "treasures"
for his nest of hoarding

A demagogue pillages
the virtues of men
to feather his nest
of control

Fourth Reich

Intoxicated with the power
to appropriate monies
for their quixotic affairs
with societal ills
self-proclaimed physicians
propose a Federal Consent Card
for the wholesale distribution
of life and death
and The People fall victim
to Doctors of Infamy

National Suicide

Pantywaist promoters
of national impotence
take the life of self-defense
by disarming The People
and wave a white flag to the world
while gun-wielding criminals
take our streets by force
and the nation is ruled
by intimidation

Assault On the Second Amendment

The public wears
a bullet-proof vest
for protection against abusers
of the right to bear arms
who murder community courage
and force the confiscation
of weapons

Political Masochism
(The Waco Massacre)

Authority
posing as political protection
searches and seizes private lives
like a marauder relentlessly attacking itself
and the public cries "Do it again!"

Premeditated Murder

Our leaders attack
God-ordained institutions
   the family
   the home
   the church
and delete the nation
from the archives of history

The Congressional Record

With scissors and glue
dishonest Congressmen
"revise and extend"
daily transcripts
of public debate
providing The People
with a "doctored" account
of Congressional proceedings
—the equivalent of a gossip tabloid—

Corruption

Wolves in Shepherd's Clothing

Senseless sheep
follow a wolf,
masquerading as a shepherd,
and faint with helplessness
at the baring of his teeth

Gullible citizens
elect a fraud,
feigning integrity,
and acquiesce
as he picks their pockets with flattery

Bought Votes

A man of God goes to Washington
to uphold the standards of righteousness
and impart the values of his constituents

He eats at the table of bribery
and regurgitates his promise of
"no compromise"

and the ballot box is sabotaged
by political hobnobbing

Den of Thieves

Thieves of power
in the den of influence
rob the Sons of Freedom
of their sovereignty
and sell immunities
as sacrificial offerings
to the gods of Special Interest

House of Ill Repute

Placing a red light in her window,
the spirit of lust
takes up residence in the White House
and while awaiting the next customer
for Presidential favors,
she prepares her bed
for a night of fornication
with the forces of
MONEY, POWER, and PASSION

(Un)Popular Vote

A President is placed
in the White House
by the Electoral College
overriding the choice
of The People

The citizens lose confidence
in the power of their vote
and boycott the election process
waiving the privilege
of self-government

Missing in Action

The will of The People
is run aground
by encroachers of personal
liberties
and no one comes to the rescue

Independence is listed
as "Missing in Action"
and the spirit
of lawful dissent
is buried at sea

Disciples of Corruption

With reckless abandon,
imperialistic lawmakers
impose rules of misconduct
upon unprincipled supporters
who dutifully live beyond their means,
look for avenues of escape,
and refuse to feel the pain of the poor

Emulating the unscrupulous
behavior of their leaders,
The People
become disciples of corruption
and The City on the Hill
is a mecca of idolatry

A Free Ride

Bloated with long-term slackers,
the Civil Service system
stifles merit,
rewards incompetence,
and sends the taxpayer the bill
for its overstated "services"

Globalism

Lost Virginity

A virgin
in the field of freedom
she had treasures
no other nation possessed
    —a purity of purpose—
    —a clarity of vision—
    —a determination of spirit—

But she lost her innocence
in the board room of globalism
and became a temple prostitute
in the mosque of materialism

Now
her purpose is defiled by appeasement
her vision is clouded by false hope
and her spirit is heavy with despair

The Melting Pot Boils

A multicultural society
stirred by the finger of "one-worldism"
removes individual distinction
melts the boundaries of separate nations
and prepares a platform for interdependence

America the Traitor

Joining pro-Arab forces
in negotiating land for peace
America puts Jerusalem
under siege
and shepherds Israel
into the sea
to guarantee an uninterrupted
flow of oil

Plutocratic Partisans
(NAFTA)

US investors
in third world politics
pay a despotic regime
to enslave its people
while forcing American taxpayers
to co-sign a loan
to rescue the Mexican peso
from a peasant uprising
and our leadership shows the world
how to do unto others
what it has done unto itself

Pledge of Treason

I pledge allegiance
to the flag
of the United Nations
of the World
and to the Common Market
for which it stands
Many countries
under one defense system
interdependent,
with freedom and democracy
relinquished by all

Preamble to the Constitution
of the New World Order

"We, the People of the global community,
in order to form a more peaceful world,
establish a universal court system,
insure a controlled environment,
provide for a joint military,
promote a common currency,
and secure the curse of Internationalism
upon ourselves and our descendants,
do ordain and establish this Constitution
for the generic population of the World."

Deception

Liberated Confusion

On the dance floor
of dialectic materialism
Russia leads
    two steps forward
    one step backward
and America follows
by disarming her missiles
believing the pressure
is off
while the persecuted flee
through the escape valve
of confusion
and a door is opened
for American investment
in the reconstruction
of the Russian economy

Disarmed

We thought the bear
had been declawed
so we invited him to entertain
our troops

His trainers assured us
his aggression was contained
when suddenly he attacked
our Commander-in-Chief

He dragged our limp body
into captivity
and the flag was flown upside-down
by the Masters of Deceit

Military Weakness

Combat Ready?

Defense Department cut-backs,
a chaplain stripped of his cross,
and a Presidential pardon
for homosexual hanky-panky
make the soldier in the foxhole
a sitting duck
for military martyrdom

Culture Shock
(The 1960s)

From a commune of passivity
the Hippie violently attacked
    the work ethic
    family values
    and social responsibility
sending shock waves of thanklessness
through a nation immersed
in guerrilla warfare
with the forces of subterfuge

Internal Conflict

A home divided
by marital tension
is made vulnerable to adulterous
relationships
and the breakup of the family unit

A nation divided
by civil unrest
is made susceptible to socialist reformers
and the breakdown of military defenses

Glory Departed
(Ichabod)

As the band played
the national anthem,
I stood to honor
Old Glory

I placed my hand
across my heart
but couldn't raise
my head

For my ears heard
another sound—
the playing of taps
over our military strength

On My Honor

Men of valor
men of power
men of proud
and humble motives

Serve their country
with their lives
and win the purple heart
of courage
from a Defense Department
that deserts
its men on the field

TWO

Humanism

Men will be lovers of self.

—2 Timothy 3:2

Deification of Man

The Takeover
(man as god)

A people stripped
of their religious heritage
weep at the casket
of free speech

The flag is folded
in three-corner precision
and handed to the closest relative
    —humanism—

May Man Prevail

Modern man
in search of a soul
submits to the conjectures
of value-free psychology
and places his unconscious mind
on the couch of transformation
to be analyzed, categorized,
and probed for childhood conflict
while having his libido measured
by the pleasure principle

Providing hope through
cultural and economic factors
neurosis and psychoses
are brought under control
in a society made sane
by a revolution of escape
And a new language is invented
for the symptoms of sin

Independence from God

A Congressional Declaration
of Independence from God
deems religion and morals
unnecessary to good government

The home is undermined
by federal assistance
and the State becomes the father
of immorality

The sanctity of life
is left to die
on the sterile
courtroom floor

People clamor
for civil rights
and blame society
for their raucous behavior

Permissive children
disdain authority
and create a sub-culture
of mob rule

And individual freedom
is shifted
to the shoulders
of totalitarianism

Intolerable Acts

The Ten Commandments
are declared unconstitutional

The Bible
is expelled from State institutions

Christmas
is renamed "a winter festival"

Nativity scenes
are removed from the public square

Prayer
is ousted from tax-supported schools

Babies in the womb
are ruled to be non-persons

School children
are equipped with the tools of promiscuity

The Puritan influence
is divorced from Thanksgiving

What the Lord giveth
the Government taketh away

Pride

America Exposed

An adulterous heart
A whoring spirit
A love of idols
An obsession with self

A nation exposed
and found wanton

National Impudence

With our pride
we provoke the anger of God

> In a land of affluence
> we complain for more

> In the lap of luxury
> we scorn those less fortunate

> At a feast of fatness
> we bite the hand that feeds us

> From a position of favor
> we presume upon His mercy

And with contempt
we spit in the face of LOVE

Icon of Pride

A child that is given
adult status
and treated as if
he can do no wrong
is made vulnerable
to a sadistic spirit
by the power he cannot handle

Likewise, a government
placed like an icon
on the mantle of pride
and vested with unlimited power
will rule with the gall
of a spoiled brat
and laugh at the pain
it inflicts

Path of Pride

Lost in evil imagination
the nation staggers
down the path of destruction
ignoring a road sign
pointing back to righteousness

With seared conscience
and a heart of greed
she saves the environment,
kills her babies,
and takes another drink of pride

Parched Soul

Like a wanderer in the desert
the soul of America
dies from thirst
for the Word of God

She longs for just one drink
from the stream of living water
just one glimpse
of the Word of life

Lost in the wilderness
of willful pride
She has forgotten
to whom she belongs

The Word Performed

The prophet was tired
His load was overwhelming
He couldn't carry his nation's
pride any longer

He laid his burden
at the feet of God
and called for divine
intervention

The pride of the people
rose up to mock
and God performed
the Word of his prophet

by aggressively attacking
their idols

Miracles of Terror
(Psalm 29)

From the ashes
of a volcanic eruption
The Voice of God Speaks

From the debris
of a devastating hurricane
The Voice of God Speaks

From the waters
of a raging flood
The Voice of God Speaks

From the flames
of a forest fire
The Voice of God Speaks

From the trembling ground
of an earthquake
The Voice of God Speaks

From the blood
of violence in the streets
The Voice of God Speaks

From the courtroom
of injustice
The Voice of God Speaks

"Your land hemorrhages
from the weight of sin.
Repent and return to Me."

The People
turn a deaf ear
and America goes belly-up

Idolatry

Misplaced Loyalty

You love the land
more than Me

You love the cities
more than the people

You love yourself
more than the land
    the people
    and Me

You are your own god

Desensitized by Idols

America has begun
to resemble her idols
    cold
    hard
    unfeeling

Desensitized by
    self-loving
    self-exalting
    self-protecting
gods of greed

She grieves for the days of
    wholesomeness
    chastity
    and sensitivity

The Closed Mind

Minds
darkened by idols
read The Word
and call for an interpreter
who finds an intellect
unreceptive
to simple truth

Graven Image
(Isaiah 40:17)

An idol stood
between God and me
and demanded
my total allegiance

I admired its beauty
Its magnificent splendor
I marveled at its wisdom
and seeming invincibility

I laid down my life
to preserve its freedom
I saluted and sang
to its honor

Then an invisible hand
pushed my idol over
and I saw it was just a reflection
of My Creator

A mere image
of the Kingdom to come

THREE

Materialism

Men will be lovers of money.

—2 Timothy 3:2

Greed

Greedy Rich Men

You control and manipulate
and orchestrate circumstances
to revolve around you
and your self-serving kingdom

You dangle your trinkets
before hungry eyes
like a fish hook baited
and ready to set

You despise the poor
for their helplessness
yet envy their simplicity
and moral resolve

Your quest to satisfy
the unmeetable need
is a vicious circle
of consuming passion

Exhausted by greed
and exploiting people
you hide your discontent
behind lonely laughter

Vertical Vision

The horizontal gate
of destruction
is open wide
and passions run wild

For a bag of money
America betrays her first love
and goes a whoring
from her God

The church points
to a vertical gate
of peace, sacrifice,
and eternal values

But The People curse God
to His face
and refuse the narrow way
of restraint

Blind Ambition

You clutch your money
to your heart
and declare your allegiance
to the Almighty Dollar

You try to buy favor
with prudence and charity
but I see your motive
of blind ambition

Your greed has become
the presiding judge
over your accountability
to God

Stone of Remembrance

A man who is
his own god
makes money to please himself
and lives for the ultimate
acquisition—
the best tombstone available
for short-sighted fools

Material Man

Eyes dart
with discontent
from money to pleasure to power
and search faces
for the look of worship
that will satisfy the craving
of an ingrown ego

Despotism

A government
that divorces
the needs of The People
robs God
and flirts
with economic collapse

Debt and Usury

Capital Offense

Inflationary spending
by undisciplined
"elected representatives"
of involuntarily surrendered
tax monies
squanders our investment
drains our capital resources
and causes us to commit
grand larceny against ourselves

Funny Money

Valueless money
based on a weightless standard
falls into the hands
of international bankers
with an eye toward global monopoly
while our currency mocks God
with the inscription
"In Usury We Trust"

The Conspiracy

The People demand
a gold-backed dollar
to restore the economic health
of the nation

Economists, bankers
and politicians
conspire to keep
the presses rolling

And the economy collapses
from instability

Regulation and Dependency

Economic Skullduggery

Villainizing profit
regulating productivity
and rationing success
Masters of economic destiny
with a vested interest in inflation
dominate supply and demand
by political pull
and create a public trough
of crisis intervention
and an economic climate
of social dependency

S & L Bailout

My neighbor bought
a house
and couldn't pay the mortgage
so the government garnished
my wages to cover his debt
and gave the maverick
economic immunity

Overconsumption

Accustomed to a grubstaked lifestyle,
spendthrift consumers
overborrow and underinvest
in the bankrupt economy
of a debtor nation
that owes more than it earns

Exploitation

Severe Lockdown

Corrupt power structures
imprison our men
in systems designed
to render them impotent

Robbed of individuality
by oppressive leadership
Trapped in a maze
of tyrannical laws

Their dream of autonomy
sits locked behind bars
while the wheels of industry
turn their sweat into gold

A Poor Mentality

Minds
freeze-branded* from birth
with the lie that IQ
is determined by family income
will be limited by an institutional
assessment of worth
and strategically pigeonholed
by state-approved saviors
of the destitute

---

*Freeze-branding is the "humane" way of branding cattle.

Involuntary Servitude

The property owner
pays for schools

The property owner
pays for cities

The property owner
pays for reservoirs

The property owner
pays for police protection

> So the poor can buy candy
> with food stamps

> Put illegitimate babies
> on the welfare rolls

> And fill our jails
> with crimes of boredom

Then the property owner
pays to incarcerate a societal parasite
while struggling to grow his land
under government control

And The People lose incentive

The Bookie

Junk Bond defaults
Leveraged takeovers
Federal buy-outs

Uncle Sam loses his shirt
in bankruptcy proceedings

Indifference

"When I Grow Up"
(Psalm 127:3)

40,000 children
die every day*
from the symptoms of poverty
    starvation
    deprivation
    despair
in nations
too poor to care

4,000 babies
die every day+
from the symptoms of prosperity
    selfishness
    depravity
    indifference
in a nation
too greedy to care

And the "heritage of the Lord"
is denied the right
to grow up

---

*Poverty statistics (Compassion International)
+Abortion statistics (National Right to Life)

Poverty

Slave Labor

They come to America
to seek their fortunes
to escape oppression
to make a better life
for their families

Most find a system
of hand-outs and dependency
more profitable
than sweat-earned
money

The honorable
work in slavery conditions
for wages below minimum
standards

And they wag their heads
in disbelief
at the death of the
"American Dream"

America's Weak Spot

A scar on the face of pride
An offense to the mannered elite
An embarrassment to a
    boondoggling bureaucracy
The Achilles' heel of a democratic society
    —the downcast eye of the homeless—

Welfare Despair

Arms hanging limp
at your side
Refusing to lift a finger
to provide

Hiding behind handouts
and inherited excuses
You shrug at "forces
beyond your control"

And produce shiftless
children
who view God as a woman

The Great Experiment

The elite wisdom
of social scientists
declares war on the poor
by providing work disincentives
and a bonus for illegitimate births

Charging the taxpayer for upkeep
on a government-sponsored whorehouse,
liberal idealists
foster a social disease
called "father flight"
and circumvent the needy's
accountability to God

Maze of Deprivation

Like mice in a maze
with no escape
ghetto dwellers
prey upon each other
and take their identity
from a restricted segment
of society

Fading Status Rewards

In the new democratic
socialistic America
the "filthy rich"
rule the "dirt poor"
and the working class
is taxed out of existence
by a government that refuses
to "buy American"

Regulation of the Poor

Regulators of the Poor
determine income,
control reproduction,
and diffuse civil unrest
with programs of relief
guaranteed to keep
the "underprivileged"
on the dole

The Gift of Poverty

A poor man gives liberally
and gets a pauper's reward
—power over a selfish heart—

FOUR

Hedonism

Men will be lovers of pleasure.

–2 Timothy 3:4

Gambling

Risky Business

A decadent society
plays away the work ethic
gambles away free enterprise
and throws away democracy
on a budget of chance

Addicted to Covetousness

Wages earned
for daily provision
are spent to appease
an inner addiction—
the compulsion
to throw money away

Families seek help
from a society
bewitched by covetousness
and discover
greed has killed
all concern for human flesh

The Lottery

Government sponsored "investment"
in unearned income
promotes the hope
of pain-free success
and undermines the prestige
of productive labor
endorsing irresponsibility as a thrill
and sanctioning poor stewardship

The Bandit

Blackjack, roulette,
horse race betting,
riverboat casinos
and one-arm bandits

Lower taxes
improved roads
the creation of jobs
tourist trade attraction

The subtle enticement
for "hands-on" participation
in the abandonment of the community
to organized crime

Money—The Toy
(Ephesians 5:16)

Money
in the hands of lust
satisfies the senses
and sets in motion
a cycle of wrath
brought about by walking
after the flesh

Pornography

Youth Cult

Pornography—the ultimate prejudice—
rejects the unattractive
for an illusion of perfection
while the mind commits incest
within the family of God
and meditates upon
never growing old

The Politics of Pornography

Wrapped in a cloak
of art, literature,
politics and science,
pornographic magazines
avoid being defined as obscene
and claim the constitutional right
to dignify deviant behavior

The Fixation

Obsessed with aberrant
sexual behavior
and the subordination and exploitation
of women and children
obscenity,
appealing to the prurient interest
and lacking any cultural value,
patently offends
the "average person's"
standard of morality
and violates individual worth

Alcohol Abuse

Intoxicated Society

Advertisements glamorizing
the social drink
create peer pressure
to anesthetize the pain of reality
with alcohol
fomenting a society
intoxicated with escapism

A Family "Disease"

Afraid of living life sober
parents numb their minds
with liquor
inflicting the family
with the "disease" of drunkenness
and making lifelong "enablers"
of their children
who search for will power
in the impotent god of psychology

Drug Abuse

Under the Influence

Leaders
under the influence
of mind altering drugs
put the community at the mercy
of unpredictable behavior
and The People
under the rulership
of evil "spirits"

Fatal Frenzy

Alcohol, marijuana
cocaine, heroin
recreational addiction
to instant insanity

Prescription pills
designer drugs
the insatiable dependence
upon tranquilization

"Mystical" hallucination
cross-addicted euphoria
torturous withdrawal
from chemical crutches

Narcotic induced
"psychotic" disorders
brain damage, paralysis
rigidity, death

A fatal fascination
with pleasure
"If it feels good,
do it"

Government Funded Destruction

Subsidized Death

The Surgeon General
declares passive smoke
to be a carcinogen

Tobacco growers
boycott restaurants
with "no smoking" policies

Consumers protest
the proposed "sin tax"
on cigarettes

Manufacturers manipulate
the amount of nicotine
to guarantee addiction

And Government subsidizes
the production
of a consumer health risk

Offensive Free Speech
(National Endowment for the Arts)

Tax dollars pay
for blasphemous art
while the entertainment industry
screams "censorship"
and uses the First Amendment
as a license
to liberalize the conscience of a nation
and lower community standards

Television Pollution

Flattery Corrupts
(Jeremiah 6:15)

Sexually suggestive advertising
brings NO BLUSH
to the face of a desensitized
viewer of promiscuity
who has been seduced
by flattery to his virility
and prostituted by
unchecked eroticism

TV— The Role Model

"Latch-key" kids
come home to television
and learn to settle conflict with violence
solve lust with infidelity
reply to frustration with cursing
and respond to obligation with escape
Thus
imitating the role model
of bizarre behavior

Denying responsibility
for delinquent behavior
the media creates heroes
of brutality and indecency
and makes our children sick
with pent-up hostility

Movie Madness

Wasteland of Tolerance

The People bow
to a god of entertainment
and submit their values
to philosophical manipulation
while being conditioned to accept
a liberal world view

Programmed to adopt
a "politically correct" bias
the mind becomes a wasteland
of tolerance
and confusion

Moral Decay

Glamorized prostitution
Legitimized perversion
Accepted adultery
Dignified divorce

Aggrandized violence
Exalted crime
Obliged illegitimacy
Approved terror

Protected obscenity
Glorified rape
Endorsed abortion
Fostered drug dependency

While adults indulge the flesh
Children are taken captive to lust
While the church compromises with immorality
Vulgarians direct the future

Video Games

Idle Potential

Cinematic stimulation
and push button fantasies
provoke aggression
against a future dwarfed
by mediocrity
and the mind idles
in neutral

Musical Despair

Prophets of Despair

The youth
hysterically worship
a musical idol
and accept his philosophy
of despair
giving money and allegiance
to the sounds of hell
and creating a monster
of vain ambition
who dies from self-inflicted
abuses

Woodstock

"Free spirits" assemble
to celebrate "peace"
and produce the "love-child"
of hopelessness

Sports Obsession

National Preoccupation

Feet pound
the pavement of time
striving to regain
lost control

Tight, tanned skin
works up a sweat
to build muscles
of self-admiration

Hands
put down the fork
and refuse to feed a body
out of shape with the world

People
preoccupied with themselves
maintain the physical
and starve the spirit

The Fame Game

Millionaire players
in the game of fame
give the public an image
that sells tickets
while practicing their vices
in secret
giving professional sports
a bad reputation
and selling their souls
for significance

New Rules of the Game

Professional athletes
with amateur emotions
break the rules of
honorable conduct
claiming exemption
by reason of depravity
and modeling the standard
of unprecedented immorality

Hero No More

A larger-than-life
sports figure
is accused of committing
a crime of passion
and the public salivates
over his media-monitored
break with reality

Greed the Winner

At the bargaining table
of greed
players pout
for unlimited earnings
and threaten owners
with poor performance
while the government
serves as umpire
in the major league game
of covetousness

Self-Indulgence

Gluttony

A leadership spoiled
by unbroken success
steals from The People
to build a house
on the sinking sand
of self-indulgence

A people
of unrestrained appetite
pollute the world
with their barbarism
and recycle their rapacity
for future generations
of gluttons

While gorging on freedom
they choke on their greed

Pleasuring

Flesh and blood
seeks gratification
in the desire to conquer
and finds intimacy
with the man in the mirror

FIVE

Nihilism

Men will be . . . boastful, arrogant, revilers, disobedi-
ent to parents, ungrateful, unholy, unloving, irreconcil-
able, malicious gossips, without self-control, haters of good,
treacherous, reckless, conceited . . .

—2 Timothy 3:2-4

General Despair and Perverted Values

Death of Dignity

Bodies exploited
by the love of money
Babies molested
by lawlessness

Motherhood demeaned
by recreational sex
Domestic tranquility threatened
by casual brutality

Morality weakened
by political apathy
The "sweet land of liberty"
is caught with her pants down

Harbinger of Premature Death
(Isaiah 5:20)

The media shuns
traditional values
and heralds
the premature death of a culture
    —the victim of its own excesses—

Calling good, evil
and evil, good
it extinguishes the torch
of journalistic integrity
and confuses the face
of the truth seeker

Family Disintegration

Age of Darkness

The word "family" is erased
from the chalkboard of America
and the nation enters
an age of darkness

The State separates
man from his authority
and substitutes programs
of control:
    Population control
    Gun control
    Environmental control
    Price control
    Educational control

And the child, seeking solidarity,
joins a gang of anarchy
bringing down
a reign of terror

Division Lowers Defenses

Divorce tears the fabric
of unity
and weakens the resolve
of The People
to withstand the elements
of adversity
leaving children to do the repairs
from a memory distorted by division
creating a military too frayed
to fight

Educational Decline

Mind Control

Children are robbed
of the blessings of liberty
by a composite education
for a world community

Posterity is sacrificed
on an ecumenical altar
of guided mental imagery,
earth worship and
divine selfhood

Ethics, patriotism,
and Christian values
are brought under the subjection
of group will

One nation
under many gods
commits the mind
as a ward of the State
and shatters its indivisibility

Conditioned by Conformity

Like pawns on a chessboard
our children yield
to the strategy of amorality
and are checkmated by conformity

Bored with legitimized sex
Conditioned to de-value life
they shock the future
with real guns

Rebellion of Children

Flight from Authority

Our children curse authority
slam the door on communion with God
shove eternal values in the closet
and raise the window to earthly pursuits
committing their minds to openness
and their bodies to demon possession

Educational Pig Sty

When God was expelled
from school
    Children became swine
    conceiving litters of bastards
    while feeding from the trough
    of humanistic slop
    and wallowing
    the Ten Commandments
    into the mud

Generation X*

Baby boomer offspring
react
to the cultural paranoia
and moral hypocrisy
of their ex-hippie turned yuppie
parents
and choose an eccentric lifestyle
of history denial

---

*The "X Generation" is the new hippie movement defined
in Douglas Coupland's book, *Generation X: Tales for an Accel-
erated Culture.*

Abortion

Lost Generation

David committed adultery
with Bathsheba
and lost the son they
had conceived

America goes to bed
with greed
and suffers a miscarrying
womb

Born Equal

Human life
is not a commodity
to be bartered for
on the auction block
of slavery

Personhood
is not a judgment
to be made
by the fall
of a courtroom gavel

Freedom
is not in "quality"
but in
"equality"

Death of a Conscience

The flag is flown at half-staff
over the womb of the nation,
robbed of innocent life
by doctors of death,
while the leaders try to hide
the blood on their hands

A Hard Pill to Swallow

A proposal is brought before Congress
to appoint an Ambassador to the unborn
for the purpose of making a peace treaty
with babies in the womb

The proposal is held up in Committee
while the President negotiates
with foreign drug companies
for the murder of maternal love

Medical Care(lessness)

The government assures
our future health
by rationing benefits,
euthanizing the old and infirm,
and aborting our God-sent answers
to disease and world starvation

Depreciation of Life

Decomposed
Standards of Conduct

Voluntary, involuntary
active, passive
Ethical acceptance
of euthanasia

Gender selection
pregnancy termination
A relative standard
for absolute infanticide

"Death with dignity"
assisted suicide
The Hippocratic Oath betrayed
by doctors of impunity

An epidemic of perversion
a politically protected disease
The willful disposal of life
by scavengers of greed

Victims of Choice

Children are killed
for the sins of their fathers,
their mothers suffer
from post-murder syndrome,
and the soul of the nation
cries dry tears

Violence

A Culture of Violence

Ill-tempered athletes
with money-based loyalties
perform olympic feats
of political grandstanding
whetting the appetites
of their gladiator-hungry fans
and doing violence to the principle
of fair play

L.A. Riots

The unethical use of force
by arrogant authoritarians
inflames deep-seated resentment
for past discriminations
and unleashes a retaliatory
spree of crime
against the confines of poverty

Acting out
their philosophy of despair
"the survival of the fittest"
The People wallow
in a cesspool of violence
and deliver our streets
to pandemonium

Feminism

Sub-Standard Equality

Women clamor
for freedom to be men
and emphatically declare
independence from God

On a soapbox of equality
they demand the right to:

desert the home
while stampeding their children
in the process

exhaust the female population
while holding up the goal
"a woman in control"

have sex outside of marriage
while receiving federal assistance
with "unplanned reproductions"

possess the pulpit
while rewriting the Bible
using sexless terms

exercise power
over life and death
while claiming equality with God

demote motherhood
to an occupation
while disfiguring the feminine mystique

And the nation suffers
from maternal deprivation

The Future—Redefined

Feminists congregate
to blaspheme God
and bow to a spirit
of Jezebel

By reinventing the family
and "reimagining" Christianity
they throw our future
to the dogs

Castrated Authority

We've put an apron
around our men
and given them
kitchen work to do

We've called them chauvinists
and power hungry pigs
We've turned our men
into women

We laugh at their strength
reject them as leaders
and kill their courage
with criticism

When we're attacked
by surprise
they'll hide in fright
disarmed by the rights
of their women!

Trying to Serve Two Masters

Women demand equal pay
and take men's jobs
for the satisfaction of usurping
authority from God
    Thus
depreciating the value
of the home
and limiting the eternal rewards
of their daughters

Objects of Pity

Claiming equal rights
for chest exposure,
angry women
bare their breasts on the street
to shame men for sexual harassment
and punish themselves
for their ability to reproduce

For Hire: A Woman for Breed

Due to the accelerated ticking
of her biological clock,
career feminist seeks assistance
from medical science
for clinical conception.
Will consider all available options,
i.e., artificial insemination,
    scientific cloning,
        invitro fertilization, etc.
Morality is not an issue.
The end justifies the means.
Call 1-800-SEL-FISH.

Homosexuality

A More Perfect Union

Sodomites come out of the closet
and infect The People
with a contagious disease
while the government protects
their inalienable right
to life, liberty and the pursuit of happiness
and jeopardizes the survival of monogamy
    the principal source
    of uncontaminated blood
    and the sanctioned form
    of procreation

AIDS
Disease of Defilement

Men sleep with men
Women with women
The Holy design for marriage
is scorned

Children are used
as objects of sodomy
Future generations
are threatened by extinction

A sexual revolution
reaps what it sows
and brings death
to the bed of defilement

While society scrambles
to cover the debt
for a handicapped
morality

Injustice

Champion of the Criminal

While politicians promise
to get tough on crime,
lawyers litigate
to make the public a victim
of criminal rights
and choose juries comprised
of like-minded lawbreakers

Equal Opportunity

Equal opportunity
guaranteed by law
makes discrimination an offense
punishable by the quota system
and the government the distributor
of success

Social Concern

Relieving responsibility
from the family,
The People put security
in a bankrupt system
and discover when they're old
that the government has no heart
and their retirement will be spent
in poverty

First Amendment Imprisoned
(Application of RICO to Abortion Protesters)

Deriving their just powers
from the consent of the governed
representatives of the people,
by the people,
and for the people
imprison dissenters for
racketeering
and jeopardize the right
to peaceably assemble

Taxation without Representation

The sweeping hand
of redistribution
subsidizes the slacker
with the sweat of the industrious

Borrows from the future
through deficit spending
and promotes the general welfare
by over taxation

A nation governed
by opulence
brings leanness
to its soul

All Work is Honorable
(Martin Luther)

Government assistance
to live in poverty
produces leeches of lethargy
who renege on family responsibility
depriving themselves of the rewards
of hard work
killing their own creativity
and giving OTHERS their burden
to provide

Weak Arm of the Law

Handicapped by a missing
arm of the law
the nation winces at phantom pain
caused by an absence of moral code

The scales of justice
are tipped toward bribery
and truth is interpreted
by politics

The prisons are a revolving door
for repeat offenders
The streets are the playground
of criminals

Due process is bogged down
in regulatory bureaucracy
while the citizens' right to redress
is a lawyer's practical joke

Judicial Mutiny

Children denied the right to pray
are taught that pride
is the salvation of mankind
and that authority answers to no one

So chaos rules the schools
anarchy rules the streets
and mutiny rules
the Supreme Court

Fundamentalism Aroused

A donkey kicks
a lion in the head
and awakens a sleeping
giant

Modernists make a mockery
of justice
and rouse the anger
of God

Court of Contempt

Lives hanging in the balance
stand before judges of disrepute

Flesh judging flesh
by a materialistic standard

Where justice
is an enemy of the court
and mercy is held in contempt

Divine Entitlement
(2 Chronicles 34)

King Josiah read
the Word of God
and the people swooned,
amazed at how far
they had strayed

Our courts
close the books
on the laws of God
and The People reel
from the extortion of their
God-given rights

Union Justice

Workers organize
for financial security
and strike a deal
with management
to forego individual initiative,
sabotage entrepreneurship,
and sacrifice the "bottom line"
to seniority

Poor Me Syndrome

Hearts allegedly hardened
by rejection
seek solace in the arms
of escapism

    drugs
    alcohol
    pornography

    gambling
    overeating
    illicit sex

and the government
considers legalizing
compulsive behavior

A Judicial System Run Amuck

An eleven-year-old girl
is raped by four men
and suffocated with her own
underwear
and the death sentence
is deemed "inhumane"

A serial killer
lies peacefully on a gurney
while being injected with a lethal dose
of painless poison
and the lawful execution is hailed
"cruel and unusual punishment"

By erring on the side of compassion
the courts condone criminal behavior
and America is judged
a hoodlum nation
by predictors of downward trends

The Case of
Fairness versus Justice

Demanders of "equality"
promote dependence upon government,
illegitimate co-habitation,
and compensation of the underprivileged
    Thus
In the name of "impartiality"
invade the privileges of
private ownership,
free enterprise,
and the right of inheritance

Laws of "fairness"
reward indolence, immorality,
and insurrection
and punish diligence,
virtue, and community concern
    Thus
Holding "justice" hostage
to human logic
and making individual responsibility
unethical

Racism

Internalized Rage

White supremist groups
behind a guise of patriotism
plot the overthrow of
perceived injustice
and organize a band of
renegade hatemongers
intent upon purifying the culture
of its "minority influence"
and the nation goes to war
against itself

Black Nationalism

Rejecting integration,
Afro-American activists,
armed with the politics
of retaliation,
divide the nation between
black and white
and stage a revolution
of revenge

Hand-Me-Down Prejudices

Skin color disputes
    over social standing
Discriminatory labels
    for ethnic origin
The culture torn
    by a war between the sexes

A society segregated by envy

Blasphemy

America Damned

Out of the heart
of presumption
the mouth speaks profanity
invoking a curse from God
upon the land
and damning America
to Hell

Arrogance

Rejected Truth

The prophet pronounces doom
upon a murderous nation
guilty of the blood
of the innocent

The people scoff
and choose a different message
A promise of peace
and self-realization

God rocks the cradle
of aborted babies
and instructs angels to dance
on the grave of America

Emptiness

Heart and Soul

People
in a rich society
cry to be filled
with purpose
and reach for an illusive
meaningful experience
that will bring peace
to a love-starved
heart

SIX

Religious Apostasy

Men will hold to a form of religion, but will deny its power.

—2 Timothy 3:5

Pantheism

Reaping the Whirlwind

Finding their security
in external influences,
citizens celebrate "Earth Day"
and worship a "Nature"
that has turned against them
—the natural result
of sowing to the wind—

Devoured by the Force

Recruits are being sought
for a new world order
under a one-world religion
with a new-age philosophy
governed by a world-wide constitution
empowered by a mystical "force"

With hypnotic powers
the nation is "cleansed"
of "undesirable religions"
while The People chant phrases
to an inner god,
look for another level of consciousness
and deliver up their land to "the devourer"

Satanism

Bewitched Society

The spirit of Lucifer
kidnaps our children
and sacrifices their lives
on the altar of barbarism

Performing a ritual
of sexual exploitation
society is indoctrinated
into a satanic sub-culture

And the church has forgotten how to exorcise

The Demon Within

Lawless men
act out the evil intents
of their hearts
upon foolish minds
deceived by demons
as the Church fornicates
with the world
and the nation goes a whoring
from her God

Occult Crime

Devil worshipers
confuse
law enforcement officials
with crimes of ritualistic abuse
and infiltrate the Church
through unsuspected people
of prominence

Sorcery

Soldiers of Fortune

Palm reading
tea leaf interpretation
fortune telling
horoscope charts

Ouija boards
extra-sensory perception
biofeedback
astral projection

Role playing fantasy games
martial arts and yoga
levitation and spiritism
spells and incantations

Water witching
dowsing rods
hypnotism
acupuncture

Magic, witchcraft
transcendental meditation
heavy metal rock music
blanking the mind

Drug addiction
alcohol abuse
sexual perversion
devil worship

The will, the mind,
and the emotions
under the influence of demons
organize an army for the Anti-christ

Strange Gospels

Self-Absorbed

A self-possessed preacher
offers a man-centered gospel
to a self-oriented culture
and gains a temporal-minded convert
to anti-Christianity

Methods of Manipulation

Claiming divine inspiration,
evangelists of self-deification
give methods to prosperity
and handles of manipulation
to hearts that worship idols,
hands that play with sin,
and minds that soak up lies
like a sponge

Pseudo Gods

Hawking a fancy-free lifestyle,
rogues of righteousness
rob The People to feed their egos
and fail the test of character

Conned by peddlers of presumption,
beguiled followers
pledge loyalty to a pseudo god
and forward their donations
to the prison

Indifference

Involuntary Manslaughter

Gentile indifference
to Jewish persecution
gave license to the genocide
of a dispossessed race

Apathy of the church
to the slaughter of the innocent
has delayed the liberation
of babies in the womb

Dual Citizenship

A nation within a nation,
The Church
fails to pass
the torch of righteousness
to future generations
putting the nation
at odds with its Creator
and losing
the blessings of liberty

Last Days Church

A lukewarm church
patronizes God
by belittling
the blood sacrifice
of His Son
and discloses its worship
as fake

Fallen Truth

The world is forced
to make hand motions
to a church
deaf to its needs

Kingdom priests
robed in righteousness
turn a cold heart
to the naked public square

The lost plead
at the feet of the blind
for a drink
of Living Water

An eagle falls
from the sky
and America loses
the war of values

The Child of Rationalization

The Church sneers
at the plight of the poor
    (as if belonging to God
    gives immunity from pain)
and points their children
to a future on Welfare
choosing the comfort
of rationalization
over the sacrifice
of almsgiving

Compromise

Gospel of Success

Disciples of compromise
flee persecution
by embracing idols
of unrestrained freedom
and accepting the enticements
of "mandated" education
"approved" tax deductions
and "allowable" religious activities

Propagating a gospel
of peace and prosperity
under the protective arm
of "social justice"
the Church bows her head
to pray to mammon
and falls asleep in the arms
of the State

Adulterated Church

Helpless to overcome
her addiction to idols
she pursues her lovers
like a prostitute for hire
enticing them to her bed
of adultery with the world
and conceives the illegitimate child
of a demonized culture

Skeleton in the Woods

Surrounded by the lushness
    of new growth
    and long-time stands
    of greenery

A skeleton leans against a tree
    with empty eyes
    hollow ears
    and a mouth riveted shut
    by the cruelty of decay

Surrounded by the evidence
    of things unseen
    and long-standing truths
    of the Word

The Church reclines in the arms of Baal
    with eyes full of things
    ears tuned to self
    and a mouth silenced
    by humanism

Man-pleasing Spirit

People serve people
making people an idol
and receive a pat on the back
for pleasing people

Corruption

Death by Defilement

Little gods
behind big pulpits
proclaim themselves wise
all powerful
and needing nothing

Steal the glory
to exalt themselves
Defile the altar of God
with their lusts
and choke off the anointing
by guile

Let Freedom Ring

Naked and barefoot
She walks a dirt road
of exile
Like a dispossessed priest
stripped of all authority
Truth has fallen
into the hands of repression
and the Liberty Bell
has ceased to ring

Misplaced Zeal

Misguided zealots
attack sin with education,
legislation and regulation
and misrepresent God's plan
of redemption through repentance

Hypocrisy

Spiritual Schizophrenia

The church divided
between God and Baal
worships with distraction

>with one hand raised in praises
>and the other hand fingering its money

>with one eye on The Word
>and the other eye on entertainment

>with one knee bowed at holy communion
>and the other knee bent before
>worldly accomplishment

With half-hearted loyalty
it invites division
and demonstrates how to be fickle

The Great Pretender

Deceit and duplicity
the tools of hypocrisy
play hide-and-seek
with commitment
and run from accountability

Victory in Persecution

The Fugitive

Ousted from politics
by the wisdom of man
religion flees
the captivity of pride
and becomes a refugee
in the Land of Freedom

Song of Joy

Religion is taken to court
for harassment
and the church is forced
underground

Deranged leaders
drink the blood of martyrs
and from the catacombs of repression
is heard the song of JOY

Held Captive

While praising her God
in the prison of oppression
the Church scrapes her cup
across the bars
and cries to be delivered

A prophet is sent to warn the nation
"Let My People Go"
The leaders laugh and declare the Church
to be the possession of the State

God sees the tears
of His Royal Priests
and decides to free them
with miracles of terror
as the mountains of arrogance are removed!

SEVEN

The Pay-Off

Do not be deceived. God cannot be mocked; for whatever a man sows, this he will also reap.

—Galatians 6:7

Bondage

Cloak of Betrayal

The home is invaded
by thieves of autonomy

Churches dance
to the tune of tax exemption

Schools rally
around the flag of globalism

Business sells our future
to foreign interests

Politicians camouflage treason
with rubber stamp promises

Neighbor spies on neighbor
Children betray parents

Freedom sits in stocks
and the State of the Union
is SLAVERY

Reveille

The trumpet sounds
a wake-up call
to a nation unprepared
for the wrath to come

The People hear
but they cannot flee
for their feet are tied
to the cares of the world

Civil Strife

Fire on the Hill

The smoke signal
of war
ascends from Capitol Hill

The drumbeat
of territorial wars
rattles the trees

The wavering siren
of a nation under siege
sounds through the streets

The People
scramble to find refuge
from the ravages of civil unrest

Fire on The Hill
destroys the vestiges
of a heritage rich in freedom

The Damage Assessment

The prey is polluted
—the curse of poor stewardship

The People lie dead in the streets
—a sacrifice to their fortress god

The land is a habitation of demons
—a memorial to the pride of man

Disease

Fatal Resistance

Bacteria that defies
all known treatment
creates a medical disaster
of global proportion
and ushers in a post-antibiotic era

Leading scientific authorities
are incapable of helping
a people
who stubbornly refuse
to fear God

Economic Collapse

Apathy

Because you allowed
evil to prosper
and did not restrain
the powers of darkness

Your children will eat bread
with trembling lips
and drink water
in fear

Their frail bodies
will be a haunting reminder
of your days of
revelry

Destruction

Buried Alive

As Jerusalem
was once desolate,
home of the jackal
    which disembowels its prey
    while still alive

So America
will be desolate
disemboweled of her pride
    and left to die
    from the shock

Land of Extinction

Death to your rivers
Death to your crops
Death to your bodies
Death to your minds
Death to your money
Death to your possessions
Death to your defenses
Death to your hope

For the blood you've shed
will be brought on your own head
and the violence you've embraced
shall be the weapon of your demise

Day of Accountability

In one day
your idols
will be smashed

In one day
the crimes you've committed
will put you in captivity

In one day
the violence you've performed
will fall on your own head

In one day
MY TRUTH
will be avenged

In one day
you shall know
that I AM GOD!

Grace Removed

A nation that continues
to commit adultery with idols
while God is screaming in its ear
"turn from your wicked ways
and live"
gives children permission
to disrespect authority
and God just cause
to remove His grace

Sodom Revisited

Standing on the edge of time
trying to escape the noises of my mind

The children cry for morality
the mothers scream—individuality
the fathers strive for immortality
the aged moan brutality

Natural disasters shake the land
blood and semen flood the streets
the rich get richer
the poor get poorer
the middle class pays for the gap

With a leadership powerless
against socialist infiltration,
we drink and breathe our own sewage
radiation leaks flesh eating cancer
the cults and occult murder innocent thousands

Gun runners, drug smugglers,
underground war
silver screen idols
the worship of youth
nudity, obscenity
vulgarity and violence
I grieve the death of our dignity

My right hand holds the past
our struggle for freedom
The left clutches the future
against self-destructed liberty

The road ahead—
sorrow and bloodshed
My eyes turn upward for hope
God save us from ourselves!

Deathwatch

Greed, violence and perversion
gnaw at the moral structure of America
and the Statue of Liberty
crumbles from within

A Prophet is sent
to keep vigil
over a nation
flirting with death

The people bind him
with cords of presumption
and cut out his tongue
with the knife of vengeance

Confirming their covenant
with death
and sealing the fate
of the nation

"And the Lord, the God of their fathers, sent word to
them again and again by His messengers, because He had
compassion on His people and on His dwelling place; but
they continually mocked the messengers of God, despised
His words and scoffed at His prophets, until the wrath of
the Lord arose against His people, until there was no
remedy."

–2 Chronicles 36:15-16

Postscript

Judgment at the Gate

Oh keeper of the gate
of judgment
Hold back your fury
a little longer

My friend has just
become a Christian
It startles her to think
of judgment right now

SHE NEEDS A GOD OF LOVE

Oh keeper of the gate
of judgment
Have mercy on my brother
who needs time to think

His daughter has cancer
and his mind is confused
He's trying to find You
in his pain

HE NEEDS A GOD OF COMPASSION

Oh keeper of the gate
of judgment
Consider my daughter
who's lost her way

She's temporarily fallen
under the spell of the world

Could you send an angel
to bring her back?

SHE NEEDS A GOD OF FORGIVENESS

Oh keeper of the gate
of judgment
The righteous mingle
with the wicked

Their roots intertwine
in a backslidden culture
eliminating individual responsibility
and weakening morality

Would you allow them to reclaim
their heritage?

THEY NEED A GOD OF RESTORATION

Oh keeper of the gate
of judgment
The Church has lost
her focus

She reclines in the pew of compromise
and lets the world grope
a blind road to Hell

Could you open her spiritual eyes?

SHE NEEDS A GOD OF POWER

The arm of justice
parts the sea of excuses
and opens the gate of judgment
upon a nation whose wound
is too deep to heal

The people howl
and lament the fate
of a nation that publicly
accepted sin

WE RECEIVED A GOD OF CHASTISEMENT

ORDER THESE HUNTINGTON HOUSE BOOKS !

	Title	Price	
_____	America: Awaiting the Verdict—Mike Fuselier	4.99	_____
_____	America Betrayed—Marlin Maddoux	6.99	_____
_____	Beyond Political Correctness—David Thibodaux	9.99	_____
_____	A Call to Manhood—David E. Long	9.99	_____
_____	Conservative, American & Jewish—Jacob Neusner	9.99	_____
_____	The Dark Side of Freemasonry—Ed Decker	9.99	_____
_____	Deadly Deception: Freemasonry—Tom McKenney	8.99	_____
_____	Don't Touch That Dial—Barbara Hattemer & Robert Showers	9.99/19.99	_____
_____	En Route to Global Occupation—Gary Kah	9.99	_____
_____	*Exposing the AIDS Scandal—Dr. Paul Cameron	7.99/2.99	_____
_____	The Extermination of Christianity—Paul Schenck	9.99	_____
_____	Freud's War with God—Jack Wright, Jr.	7.99	_____
_____	Goddess Earth—Samantha Smith	9.99	_____
_____	Gays & Guns—John Eidsmoe	7.99/14.99	_____
_____	Heresy Hunters—Jim Spencer	8.99	_____
_____	Hidden Dangers of the Rainbow—Constance Cumbey	9.99	_____
_____	Hitler and the New Age—Bob Rosio	9.99	_____
_____	Homeless in America—Jeremy Reynalds	9.99	_____
_____	How to Homeschool (Yes, You!)—Julia Toto	4.99	_____
_____	Hungry for God—Larry E. Myers	9.99	_____
_____	*Inside the New Age Nightmare—Randall Baer	9.99/2.99	_____
_____	A Jewish Conservative Looks at Pagan America—Don Feder	9.99/19.99	_____
_____	A Journey into Darkness—Stephen Arrington	9.99	_____
_____	Kinsey, Sex and Fraud—Dr. Judith A. Reisman & Edward Eichel (Hard cover)	11.99	_____
_____	The Liberal Contradiction—Dale A. Berryhill	9.99	_____
_____	Legalized Gambling—John Eidsmoe	7.99	_____
_____	Loyal Opposition—John Eidsmoe	8.99	_____
_____	The Media Hates Conservatives—Dale A. Berryhill	9.99	_____
_____	Out of Control—Brenda Scott	9.99	_____
_____	Please Tell Me—Tom McKenney	9.99	_____
_____	Political Correctness—David Thibodaux	9.99	_____
_____	*The Question of Freemasonry—Ed Decker	2.99	_____
_____	Resurrecting the Third Reich—Richard Terrell	9.99	_____
_____	"Soft Porn" Plays Hardball—Dr. Judith A. Reisman	8.99/16.99	_____
_____	Subtle Serpent—Darylann Whitemarsh & Bill Reisman	9.99	_____
_____	*To Moroni With Love—Ed Decker	2.99	_____
_____	Trojan Horse—Brenda Scott & Samantha Smith	9.99	_____
_____	When the Wicked Seize a City—Chuck & Donna McIlhenny with Frank York	9.99	_____

Available in Salt Series   Shipping & Handling _____
                                              TOTAL _____

AVAILABLE AT BOOKSTORES EVERYWHERE or order direct from:
Huntington House Publishers•P.O. Box 53788•Lafayette, LA 70505
Send check/money order. For faster service use VISA/MASTERCARD
Call toll-free 1-800-749-4009.
Add: Freight and handling, $3.50 for the first book ordered, and $.50 for
each additional book up to 5 books.

Enclosed is $_____including postage.
VISA/MASTERCARD #_____ Exp. Date _____
Name_____ Phone: (   )_____
Address_____
City, State, Zip_____